Veterinarians
In Our Community

Michelle Ames

PowerKiDS press.

New York

Published in 2010 by The Rosen Publishing Group, Inc.
29 East 21st Street, New York, NY 10010

First Edition

Editor: Nicole Pristash
Book Design: Greg Tucker
Photo Researcher: Jessica Gerweck

Photo Credits: Cover, p. 17 Stewart Cohen/Pam Ostrow/Getty Images; pp. 5, 13 © www.iStockphoto.com/Willie B. Thomas; p. 7 © Roberto Della Vite/age fotostock; pp. 9, 19, 24 (center), 24 (right) Shutterstock.com; pp. 11, 21, 24 (left) © Richard Hutchings/Corbis; p. 15 Dean Golja/Getty Images; p. 23 © Juniors Bildarchiv/age fotostock.

Library of Congress Cataloging-in-Publication Data

Ames, Michelle.
   Veterinarians in our community / Michelle Ames. — 1st ed.
       p. cm. — (On the job)
   Includes index.
   ISBN 978-1-4042-8071-7 (library binding) — ISBN 978-1-4358-2457-7 (pbk.) —
ISBN 978-1-4358-2460-7 (6-pack)
   1. Veterinarians—Juvenile literature. 2. Veterinary medicine—Juvenile literature. I. Title.
   SF756.A44 2010
   636.089'0695—dc22
                                        2008052682

Manufactured in the United States of America

Contents

A veterinarian, or vet, helps animals that are hurt or sick.

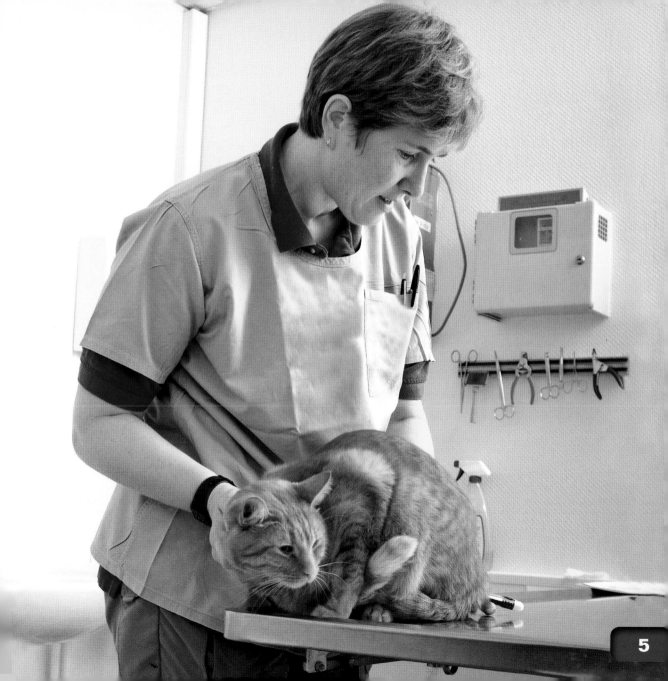

A vet works in an office. A vet's office has tables on which animals sit.

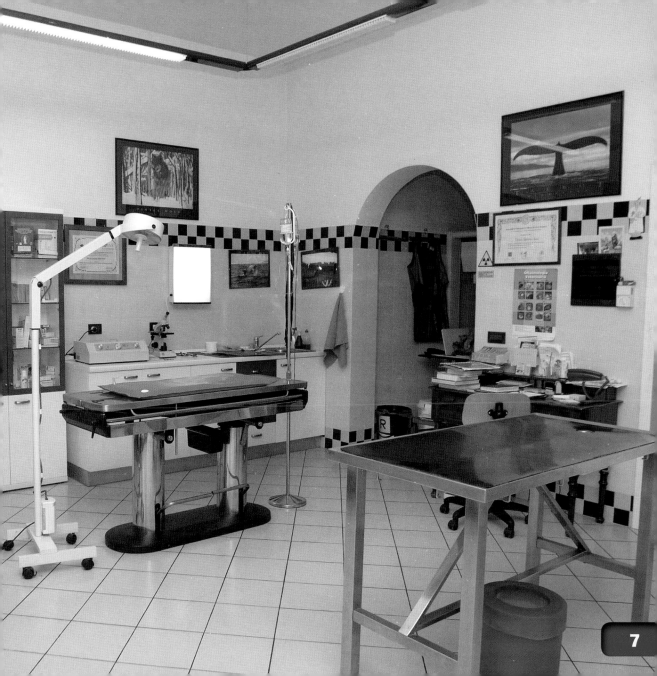

A vet checks a dog's eyesight at a checkup.

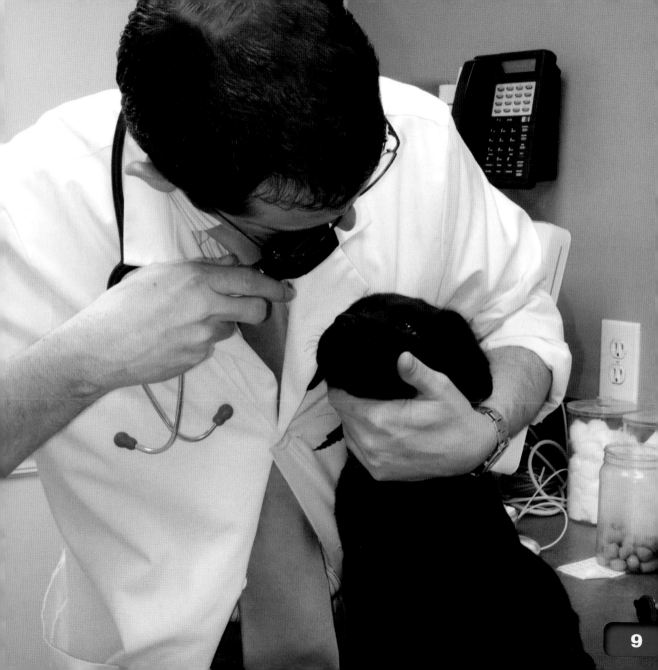

Vets often weigh animals to make sure they are healthy.

A vet looks for **fleas** in a dog's fur. Fleas make an animal itch.

This vet is listening to a rabbit's heartbeat.

A vet looks at a dog's teeth to see if its teeth are healthy.

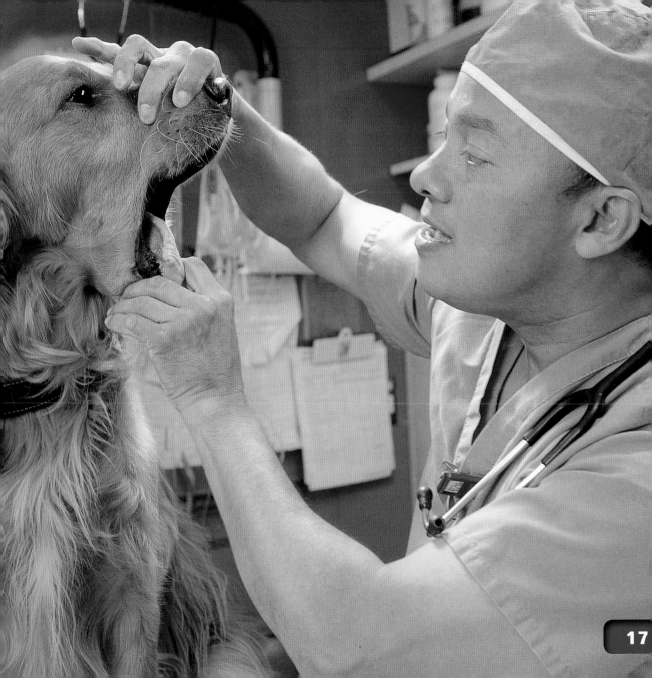

Sometimes, a dog's teeth are not healthy. A vet may need to **operate** to fix them.

This dog has hurt its leg. The vet is using a **bandage** to make it better.

Some vets work on farm animals. This vet is taking care of a donkey.

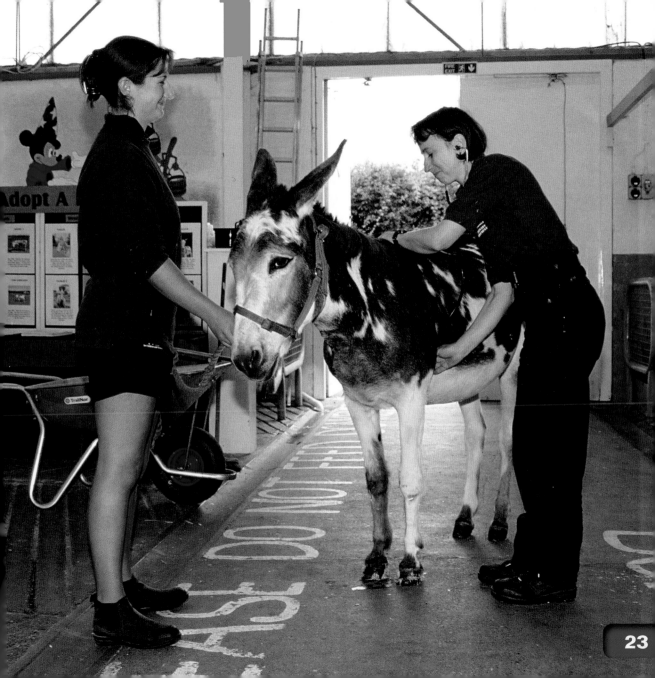

Words to Know

bandage

flea

operate

Index

Web Sites

Due to the changing nature of Internet links, PowerKids Press has developed an online list of Web sites related to the subject of this book. This site is updated regularly. Please use this link to access the list:

www.powerkidslinks.com/job/vet/